Dedicated to all my Clients, Students & Members

of our Programs around the world.

You are a constant inspiration and a reason for me

to be forever Grateful. Thank you!

DUANE ALLEY

Copyright © 2013 by Duane Alley – http://www.duanealley.com

All rights reserved. No part of this book may be produced or utilised in any form or by any means, electronic or mechanical, including photocopying, recording or by any information storage and retrieval system, without permission in writing from the Publisher.

Published 2013

Publisher: Performance Results Pty Ltd t/as Performance Results Publishing

Graphic Design & Layout: Mélissa Caron – Go-Enki.com
Editor: Richard Burian – Richard-Burian.com

Self Help

ISBN 978-0-9870571-7-4

TABLE OF CONTENTS

INTRODUCTION 9
- How the Process Works 12
- Why Would You Do This? 12
- Perceptions Change Slowly 13
- Do It Again 13

PREPARATION 15
- Deciding to Act 17
- The Seven Minute Secrets to Waking Up Better Every Day 19
- Gratitude for Things 21
- Gratitude for Others 23
- The Inner Game of Excellence 24
- The Power of Focus 24
- The Gift of Gratitude 25

JOURNAL PAGES 27

ABOUT THE AUTHOR: DUANE ALLEY 229

······· introduction ·······

WHERE TO BEGIN?

introduction :
— WHERE TO BEGIN —

This *Journey Book* serves two purposes. One, to provide readers of my *Seven Secret Habits of Success* book a place to record their passage through *The Gift of Gratitude* on a daily basis, for six months. Second, even if you haven't read my book (and I highly recommend you do – it's really good), this Journal stands alone as a useful place to record information that you need to become a better you throughout the next six months.

The purpose of completing the *Journey Book* pages every day is to give you a window into the bigger picture of how gratitude can shape your life. Understanding gratitude is one of the key parts to a successful life and career and it is only by consistently practicing it on a daily basis that we can become more consciously aware of what we can be grateful for in life and the power of that gratitude.

Your mind is a muscle; strengthen it by practicing it and learning to use it. By the same token, the more you practice gratitude, the easier it will be to accept all the blessings in life.

— How the Process Works —

So how exactly does this work? How do you, on a daily basis, become more and more thankful for the things in your life? And furthermore, what benefits will this bring you and those around you? What benefits to your family, friends, colleagues, clients and everyone else? How will becoming more aware of the things to be grateful for in your life spur you to greater and more powerful things that lead you ever closer to your goals, dreams and aspirations?

The process is rather simple; you do two things:

1) When you wake up, **write down three things, people or moments in your journal that you are most grateful for from your entire life's journey.**

2) Before you go to sleep, **write down three things, people or moments in your journal that you are especially grateful for from that day.**

— Why Would You Do This? —

Many people's views of their situation are tainted by the significance that they put on the 'bad moments'. There are always good moments as well; in fact there are probably thousands of them every week. But people selectively filter out information on a daily basis. Even in relationships, many people will take for granted when someone is doing a good job and only focus on when they make mistakes.

The journey of discovering the *Gift of Gratitude* is one of becoming a better leader, a better partner, a better parent, a better teacher and living a better life.

— Perceptions Change Slowly —

Pay attention to the slight differences and nuances in the things you are thankful and grateful for. Pay attention to the patterns that might be emerging in your thinking and also the changes that are taking place in your mindset and the things you are concerned about and thankful for.

— Do It Again —

This *Journey Book* is also useful to come back to at a later stage in your life. This book will be a record of your journey over the next six months. Don't stop there; instead, begin a life long habit of allowing yourself to record your journey and continue to focus your gratitude.

·············· preparation ··············

DECIDING TO ACT

preparation :
— DECIDING TO ACT —

Before you begin working in this *Journey Book*, it is important to make a note about decisions. The most powerful thing you can do to get started improving any area of your life is to simply make a decision.

The trick is to remember the following process whenever you are faced with the prospect of making a decision. Answering these questions will help you understand why you want to do the task you have set out and will give you the impetus to begin. The method can be called D^3 (D-Cubed):

1. Decide to do something.

2. Get determined; by realising why this is critically important to you.

3. Do it.

To get started making decisions and acting on them, fill out the following information before you start anything else in this book:

1. Decide now that you will complete the exercises in this book for the next six months.

2. Determine why it is critically important for you to fill out this *Journey Book*.

3. Do it and get started now.

— The Seven Minute Secrets —
to Waking Up Better Every Day

In my book the *Seven Minute Secrets to a Successful Life and Career*, I discuss a method that can be used every morning to help you while you complete your *Journey Book*. The trick to waking up is not as difficult as most people might think. The answer is in HOW we wake up and what we do directly after the bed. You may have heard the saying, "woke up on the wrong side of the bed" out of jest, but this is a truism and more real than people think. Your attitude directly after you wake up has the power to affect the rest of your day.

If you are like most people and you have difficulty remembering what to do as soon as you wake up, that's where this *Journey Book* comes in. Leave it by your bed and also print out the *Seven Minute Secrets* page, put it up by your bed to remind yourself to go through it every morning.

— This is what you do: —

1. Wake up whenever you do. **When you know you are awake, maybe even before you open your eyes do ONE thing – SMILE.**

2. Keep smiling and STRETCH a little – **like a cat waking up from a nap.**
   > *Stretch: Most people do not take stretching too seriously, but it can have a very positive effect on muscles that have been cramped and sore all night. Stretching when you wake up allows you to shake out those muscles and you will have less physical stress during the day when you wake up.*

3. Keep smiling and while you do your little stretch – OUT LOUD say the words "THANK YOU." – quiet, loud, full voice or whispered – doesn't matter. All that matters is that you say it.

4. LEAVE your phone OFF for at least the first hour you are awake.
   > *Phones: You might be very busy and you might need to leave your phone on, but in most cases people can afford to take at least an uninterrupted hour for themselves before they begin interacting with others.*

5. Wake, Smile, Stretch, Thank You. No phone... time to get up – AND begin the day. If you can look outside, find just one thing that is beautiful in what you see. Then find one thing that is beautiful inside. Find two things that are beautiful inside if you cannot look outside for whatever reason.

6. You're now up so get a drink of water at room temperature.
   > *Drinking Water: When you wake up, your heart rate is lower than usual and your blood is pumping more slowly, therefore bringing less oxygen to different parts of your body. Because your brain is not yet fully oxygenated, drinking a glass of water quickly spurs things into action and helps you able to focus quicker and shake off the drowsiness.*

7. Time to begin your day.

— Gratitude for Things —

Throughout this book, you will also begin to feel gratitude for more and more things. Start out in the beginning by writing down three things you are grateful for in your life. Do this now:

1. Grab a pen.

2. Write down 3 things you are GRATEFUL FOR in your life:

   > _____

   > _____

   > _____

3. Decide – Get Determined – Do It.

In the beginning, you may notice that the things you are thankful for are rather trivial. For others, they start off with rather serious things to be thankful for. Wherever you are in your journey, you will begin to notice after a few weeks or months that the things you are thankful for are changing.

Always stop to think and reflect about how you are changing as you work through this book.

— GRATITUDE FOR OTHERS —

Throughout this *Journey Book*, as you work through each month, write down three people you are grateful for. Do this now and identify three people in your life that you are grateful for when you are starting out this book. Write down who you want to thank, the reason that you will thank them for, and when you are going to do it.

1. Grab a pen.

2. Write down 3 people you want to THANK for whatever reason. Write down who you want to thank and for what reason & WHEN you will do it.

3. Commit – Plan – Do.

Gift of Gratitude Journey — Duane Alley

— The Inner Game of Excellence —

"It is all to plan; and the plan is good."

One of the biggest secrets to developing habits of success, and the one that brings many other secrets together, is the idea of maintaining an "inner game of excellence". Essentially, you are playing a game in your head – congratulating yourself at every turn, celebrating victories, setting objectives and kicking your own butt to do them. Nobody else can help you with success and achievement; it is an inner job that is created by developing new strategies to perform well.

Your results do not even have to be "great" as well. Everyone's reality is determined by the relationship between their expectations and their possibilities. The reason why you should play this inner game is to be able to perform at your highest. To do this, your inner game has to be at its peak as well. There's no point training for an athletics competition for five years and then wondering why you are not able to win against the weightlifters. It is important to ensure that your inner game is in alignment with your outer strategies to create true success.

— The Power of Focus —

The *Inner Game of Excellence* is made up of two components. The first of these are what I call the 'Power of Focus'. There are many situations where the people involved all have a different recollection of what actually took place. When people are getting on with their lives and not particularly focussed on anything, recollections of specific events can be extraordinarily different, with huge contradictions even in some of the basic facts involved. This is not exclusive to negative experiences. If you are having a positive experience (for instance at a party you really like), others might feel differently about the evening if you ask them about it. Another person's experience might be radically different to yours; even potentially a terrible one.

How does this happen? Simple – different people focussed on different things. *What we focus on not only affects our experience; it creates it.*

The key to remember here is that what we focus on doesn't create the situation; it only dictates our experience of it. Choose to focus on the negative and disempowering and that is what you will find at every turn. Instead, look out for the positive and affirming and you will be gifted and blessed with exactly this.

It's important to realise this won't stop the 'bad stuff' happening; you will however be far better equipped to deal with whatever comes along.

— The Gift of Gratitude —

The second is what I call the *Gift of Gratitude*. This is a very special type of focus and it truly is a gift for each of us. It is also a choice that we can make moment to moment. We get to decide to choose to see the blessing in the situations that happen to us. It is not only a choice to see the positive though, but rather to be active in our appreciation on that positive and the flow on affect it can, will and does have on our lives and the lives of those around us.

······· **month 1** ·······

JOURNEY PAGES

START
DATE:

DAY 1

THIS MORNING, I am grateful for :

1. _____
   _____
   _____

2. _____
   _____
   _____

3. _____
   _____
   _____

THIS EVENING, I am grateful for :

1. _____
   _____
   _____

2. _____
   _____
   _____

3. _____
   _____
   _____

••

DAY 2

THIS MORNING, I am grateful for :

1. _____

2. _____

3. _____

THIS EVENING, I am grateful for :

1. _____

2. _____

3. _____

DAY 3

THIS MORNING, I am grateful for :

1.

2.

3.

THIS EVENING, I am grateful for :

1.

2.

3.

● ●

DAY 4

THIS MORNING, I am grateful for :

1. _____
   _____
   _____

2. _____
   _____
   _____

3. _____
   _____
   _____

THIS EVENING, I am grateful for :

1. _____
   _____
   _____

2. _____
   _____
   _____

3. _____
   _____
   _____

••

DAY 5

THIS MORNING, I am grateful for :

1.

2.

3.

THIS EVENING, I am grateful for :

1.

2.

3.

DAY 6

THIS MORNING, I am grateful for :

1. _____
   _____
   _____

2. _____
   _____
   _____

3. _____
   _____
   _____

THIS EVENING, I am grateful for :

1. _____
   _____
   _____

2. _____
   _____
   _____

3. _____
   _____
   _____

DAY 7

THIS MORNING, I am grateful for :

1.

2.

3.

THIS EVENING, I am grateful for :

1.

2.

3.

DAY 8

THIS MORNING, I am grateful for :

1. _____
   _____
   _____

2. _____
   _____
   _____

3. _____
   _____
   _____

THIS EVENING, I am grateful for :

1. _____
   _____
   _____

2. _____
   _____
   _____

3. _____
   _____
   _____

DAY 9

THIS MORNING, I am grateful for :

1.

2.

3.

THIS EVENING, I am grateful for :

1.

2.

3.

DAY 10

THIS MORNING, I am grateful for :

1. _____

2. _____

3. _____

THIS EVENING, I am grateful for :

1. _____

2. _____

3. _____

DAY 11

THIS MORNING, I am grateful for :

1.

2.

3.

THIS EVENING, I am grateful for :

1.

2.

3.

DAY 12

THIS MORNING, I am grateful for :

1.

2.

3.

THIS EVENING, I am grateful for :

1.

2.

3.

DAY 13

THIS MORNING, I am grateful for :

1.

2.

3.

THIS EVENING, I am grateful for :

1.

2.

3.

• •

DAY 14

THIS MORNING, I am grateful for :

1.

2.

3.

THIS EVENING, I am grateful for :

1.

2.

3.

DAY 15

THIS MORNING, I am grateful for :

1.

2.

3.

THIS EVENING, I am grateful for :

1.

2.

3.

DAY 16

THIS MORNING, I am grateful for :

1. _____

2. _____

3. _____

THIS EVENING, I am grateful for :

1. _____

2. _____

3. _____

DAY 17

THIS MORNING, I am grateful for :

1.

2.

3.

THIS EVENING, I am grateful for :

1.

2.

3.

DAY 18

THIS MORNING, I am grateful for :

1.

2.

3.

THIS EVENING, I am grateful for :

1.

2.

3.

DAY 19

THIS MORNING, I am grateful for :

1.

2.

3.

THIS EVENING, I am grateful for :

1.

2.

3.

DAY 20

THIS MORNING, I am grateful for :

1. _____
_____
_____

2. _____
_____
_____

3. _____
_____
_____

THIS EVENING, I am grateful for :

1. _____
_____
_____

2. _____
_____
_____

3. _____
_____
_____

DAY 21

THIS MORNING, I am grateful for :

1.

2.

3.

THIS EVENING, I am grateful for :

1.

2.

3.

DAY 22

THIS MORNING, I am grateful for :

1.

2.

3.

THIS EVENING, I am grateful for :

1.

2.

3.

DAY 23

THIS MORNING, I am grateful for :

1.

2.

3.

THIS EVENING, I am grateful for :

1.

2.

3.

DAY 24

THIS MORNING, I am grateful for :

1.

2.

3.

THIS EVENING, I am grateful for :

1.

2.

3.

DAY 25

THIS MORNING, I am grateful for :

1.

2.

3.

THIS EVENING, I am grateful for :

1.

2.

3.

••

DAY 26

THIS MORNING, I am grateful for :

1. _____
   _____
   _____

2. _____
   _____
   _____

3. _____
   _____
   _____

THIS EVENING, I am grateful for :

1. _____
   _____
   _____

2. _____
   _____
   _____

3. _____
   _____
   _____

DAY 27

THIS MORNING, I am grateful for :

1.

2.

3.

THIS EVENING, I am grateful for :

1.

2.

3.

DAY 28

THIS MORNING, I am grateful for :

1.

2.

3.

THIS EVENING, I am grateful for :

1.

2.

3.

DAY 29

THIS MORNING, I am grateful for :

1.

2.

3.

THIS EVENING, I am grateful for :

1.

2.

3.

••

DAY 30

THIS MORNING, I am grateful for :

1.

2.

3.

THIS EVENING, I am grateful for :

1.

2.

3.

.... **month 2** ....

JOURNEY PAGES

START DATE:

DAY 1

THIS MORNING, I am grateful for :

1.

2.

3.

THIS EVENING, I am grateful for :

1.

2.

3.

DAY 2

THIS MORNING, I am grateful for :

1.

2.

3.

THIS EVENING, I am grateful for :

1.

2.

3.

DAY 3

THIS MORNING, I am grateful for :

1.

2.

3.

THIS EVENING, I am grateful for :

1.

2.

3.

DAY 4

THIS MORNING, I am grateful for :

1. _____
_____
_____

2. _____
_____
_____

3. _____
_____
_____

THIS EVENING, I am grateful for :

1. _____
_____
_____

2. _____
_____
_____

3. _____
_____
_____

DAY 5

THIS MORNING, I am grateful for :

1.

2.

3.

THIS EVENING, I am grateful for :

1.

2.

3.

DAY 6

THIS MORNING, I am grateful for :

1. _____

2. _____

3. _____

THIS EVENING, I am grateful for :

1. _____

2. _____

3. _____

DAY 7

THIS MORNING, I am grateful for :

1.

2.

3.

THIS EVENING, I am grateful for :

1.

2.

3.

••

DAY 8

THIS MORNING, I am grateful for :

1.

2.

3.

THIS EVENING, I am grateful for :

1.

2.

3.

DAY 9

THIS MORNING, I am grateful for :

1.

2.

3.

THIS EVENING, I am grateful for :

1.

2.

3.

DAY 10

THIS MORNING, I am grateful for :

1. _____
   _____
   _____

2. _____
   _____
   _____

3. _____
   _____
   _____

THIS EVENING, I am grateful for :

1. _____
   _____
   _____

2. _____
   _____
   _____

3. _____
   _____
   _____

DAY 11

THIS MORNING, I am grateful for :

1.

2.

3.

THIS EVENING, I am grateful for :

1.

2.

3.

DAY 12

THIS MORNING, I am grateful for :

1. _____
   _____
   _____

2. _____
   _____
   _____

3. _____
   _____
   _____

THIS EVENING, I am grateful for :

1. _____
   _____
   _____

2. _____
   _____
   _____

3. _____
   _____
   _____

DAY 13

THIS MORNING, I am grateful for :

1.

2.

3.

THIS EVENING, I am grateful for :

1.

2.

3.

DAY 14

THIS MORNING, I am grateful for :

1. _____
   _____
   _____

2. _____
   _____
   _____

3. _____
   _____
   _____

THIS EVENING, I am grateful for :

1. _____
   _____
   _____

2. _____
   _____
   _____

3. _____
   _____
   _____

DAY 15

THIS MORNING, I am grateful for :

1.

2.

3.

THIS EVENING, I am grateful for :

1.

2.

3.

••

DAY 16

THIS MORNING, I am grateful for :

1.

2.

3.

THIS EVENING, I am grateful for :

1.

2.

3.

DAY 17

THIS MORNING, I am grateful for :

1.

2.

3.

THIS EVENING, I am grateful for :

1.

2.

3.

DAY 18

THIS MORNING, I am grateful for :

1.

2.

3.

THIS EVENING, I am grateful for :

1.

2.

3.

DAY 19

THIS MORNING, I am grateful for :

1.

2.

3.

THIS EVENING, I am grateful for :

1.

2.

3.

DAY 20

THIS MORNING, I am grateful for :

1.

2.

3.

THIS EVENING, I am grateful for :

1.

2.

3.

DAY 21

THIS MORNING, I am grateful for :

1.

2.

3.

THIS EVENING, I am grateful for :

1.

2.

3.

DAY 22

THIS MORNING, I am grateful for :

1. _____
   _____

2. _____
   _____

3. _____
   _____

THIS EVENING, I am grateful for :

1. _____
   _____

2. _____
   _____

3. _____
   _____

DAY 23

THIS MORNING, I am grateful for :

1.

2.

3.

THIS EVENING, I am grateful for :

1.

2.

3.

DAY 24

THIS MORNING, I am grateful for :

1. _____
   _____
   _____

2. _____
   _____
   _____

3. _____
   _____
   _____

THIS EVENING, I am grateful for :

1. _____
   _____
   _____

2. _____
   _____
   _____

3. _____
   _____
   _____

DAY 25

THIS MORNING, I am grateful for :

1.

2.

3.

THIS EVENING, I am grateful for :

1.

2.

3.

DAY 26

THIS MORNING, I am grateful for :

1.

2.

3.

THIS EVENING, I am grateful for :

1.

2.

3.

DAY 27

THIS MORNING, I am grateful for :

1.

2.

3.

THIS EVENING, I am grateful for :

1.

2.

3.

DAY 28

THIS MORNING, I am grateful for :

1. _____
   _____
   _____

2. _____
   _____
   _____

3. _____
   _____
   _____

THIS EVENING, I am grateful for :

1. _____
   _____
   _____

2. _____
   _____
   _____

3. _____
   _____
   _____

DAY 29

THIS MORNING, I am grateful for :

1.

2.

3.

THIS EVENING, I am grateful for :

1.

2.

3.

DAY 30

THIS MORNING, I am grateful for :

1.

2.

3.

THIS EVENING, I am grateful for :

1.

2.

3.

······················· **month 3** ·······················

JOURNEY
PAGES

START DATE:

DAY 1

THIS MORNING, I am grateful for :

1.

2.

3.

THIS EVENING, I am grateful for :

1.

2.

3.

DAY 2

THIS MORNING, I am grateful for :

1. _____
_____
_____

2. _____
_____
_____

3. _____
_____
_____

THIS EVENING, I am grateful for :

1. _____
_____
_____

2. _____
_____
_____

3. _____
_____
_____

DAY 3

THIS MORNING, I am grateful for :

1.

2.

3.

THIS EVENING, I am grateful for :

1.

2.

3.

DAY 4

THIS MORNING, I am grateful for :

1.

2.

3.

THIS EVENING, I am grateful for :

1.

2.

3.

DAY 5

THIS MORNING, I am grateful for :

1.

2.

3.

THIS EVENING, I am grateful for :

1.

2.

3.

DAY 6

THIS MORNING, I am grateful for :

1. _____
   _____
   _____

2. _____
   _____
   _____

3. _____
   _____
   _____

THIS EVENING, I am grateful for :

1. _____
   _____
   _____

2. _____
   _____
   _____

3. _____
   _____
   _____

DAY 7

THIS MORNING, I am grateful for :

1.

2.

3.

THIS EVENING, I am grateful for :

1.

2.

3.

DAY 8

THIS MORNING, I am grateful for :

1. _____

2. _____

3. _____

THIS EVENING, I am grateful for :

1. _____

2. _____

3. _____

DAY 9

THIS MORNING, I am grateful for :

1.

2.

3.

THIS EVENING, I am grateful for :

1.

2.

3.

DAY 10

THIS MORNING, I am grateful for :

1.

2.

3.

THIS EVENING, I am grateful for :

1.

2.

3.

DAY 11

THIS MORNING, I am grateful for :

1.

2.

3.

THIS EVENING, I am grateful for :

1.

2.

3.

DAY 12

THIS MORNING, I am grateful for :

1.

2.

3.

THIS EVENING, I am grateful for :

1.

2.

3.

DAY 13

THIS MORNING, I am grateful for :

1.

2.

3.

THIS EVENING, I am grateful for :

1.

2.

3.

DAY 14

THIS MORNING, I am grateful for :

1.

2.

3.

THIS EVENING, I am grateful for :

1.

2.

3.

DAY 15

THIS MORNING, I am grateful for :

1.

2.

3.

THIS EVENING, I am grateful for :

1.

2.

3.

DAY 16

THIS MORNING, I am grateful for :

1.

2.

3.

THIS EVENING, I am grateful for :

1.

2.

3.

DAY 17

THIS MORNING, I am grateful for :

1.

2.

3.

THIS EVENING, I am grateful for :

1.

2.

3.

DAY 18

THIS MORNING, I am grateful for :

1.

2.

3.

THIS EVENING, I am grateful for :

1.

2.

3.

DAY 19

THIS MORNING, I am grateful for :

1.

2.

3.

THIS EVENING, I am grateful for :

1.

2.

3.

DAY 20

THIS MORNING, I am grateful for :

1.

2.

3.

THIS EVENING, I am grateful for :

1.

2.

3.

DAY 21

THIS MORNING, I am grateful for :

1.

2.

3.

THIS EVENING, I am grateful for :

1.

2.

3.

DAY 22

THIS MORNING, I am grateful for :

1.

2.

3.

THIS EVENING, I am grateful for :

1.

2.

3.

DAY 23

THIS MORNING, I am grateful for :

1.

2.

3.

THIS EVENING, I am grateful for :

1.

2.

3.

• •

DAY 24

THIS MORNING, I am grateful for :

1.

2.

3.

THIS EVENING, I am grateful for :

1.

2.

3.

DAY 25

THIS MORNING, I am grateful for :

1.

2.

3.

THIS EVENING, I am grateful for :

1.

2.

3.

DAY 26

THIS MORNING, I am grateful for :

1. _____
   _____
   _____

2. _____
   _____
   _____

3. _____
   _____
   _____

THIS EVENING, I am grateful for :

1. _____
   _____
   _____

2. _____
   _____
   _____

3. _____
   _____
   _____

DAY 27

THIS MORNING, I am grateful for :

1.

2.

3.

THIS EVENING, I am grateful for :

1.

2.

3.

DAY 28

THIS MORNING, I am grateful for:

1.

2.

3.

THIS EVENING, I am grateful for:

1.

2.

3.

DAY 29

THIS MORNING, I am grateful for :

1.

2.

3.

THIS EVENING, I am grateful for :

1.

2.

3.

DAY 30

THIS MORNING, I am grateful for :

1.

2.

3.

THIS EVENING, I am grateful for :

1.

2.

3.

.... **month 4** ....

JOURNEY PAGES

START
DATE:

DAY 1

THIS MORNING, I am grateful for :

1.

2.

3.

THIS EVENING, I am grateful for :

1.

2.

3.

••

DAY 2

THIS MORNING, I am grateful for :

1. _____
_____
_____

2. _____
_____
_____

3. _____
_____
_____

THIS EVENING, I am grateful for :

1. _____
_____
_____

2. _____
_____
_____

3. _____
_____
_____

DAY 3

THIS MORNING, I am grateful for :

1. _____

2. _____

3. _____

THIS EVENING, I am grateful for :

1. _____

2. _____

3. _____

DAY 4

THIS MORNING, I am grateful for :

1.

2.

3.

THIS EVENING, I am grateful for :

1.

2.

3.

DAY 5

THIS MORNING, I am grateful for :

1.

2.

3.

THIS EVENING, I am grateful for :

1.

2.

3.

DAY 6

THIS MORNING, I am grateful for :

1.

2.

3.

THIS EVENING, I am grateful for :

1.

2.

3.

DAY 7

THIS MORNING, I am grateful for :

1.

2.

3.

THIS EVENING, I am grateful for :

1.

2.

3.

• •

DAY 8

THIS MORNING, I am grateful for :

1.

2.

3.

THIS EVENING, I am grateful for :

1.

2.

3.

DAY 9

THIS MORNING, I am grateful for :

1.

2.

3.

THIS EVENING, I am grateful for :

1.

2.

3.

• •

DAY 10

THIS MORNING, I am grateful for :

1.

2.

3.

THIS EVENING, I am grateful for :

1.

2.

3.

DAY 11

THIS MORNING, I am grateful for :

1.

2.

3.

THIS EVENING, I am grateful for :

1.

2.

3.

DAY 12

THIS MORNING, I am grateful for :

1. _____

2. _____

3. _____

THIS EVENING, I am grateful for :

1. _____

2. _____

3. _____

DAY 13

THIS MORNING, I am grateful for :

1.

2.

3.

THIS EVENING, I am grateful for :

1.

2.

3.

••

DAY 14

THIS MORNING, I am grateful for :

1.

2.

3.

THIS EVENING, I am grateful for :

1.

2.

3.

DAY 15

THIS MORNING, I am grateful for :

1.

2.

3.

THIS EVENING, I am grateful for :

1.

2.

3.

DAY 16

THIS MORNING, I am grateful for :

1.

2.

3.

THIS EVENING, I am grateful for :

1.

2.

3.

DAY 17

THIS MORNING, I am grateful for :

1.

2.

3.

THIS EVENING, I am grateful for :

1.

2.

3.

DAY 18

THIS MORNING, I am grateful for :

1.

2.

3.

THIS EVENING, I am grateful for :

1.

2.

3.

DAY 19

THIS MORNING, I am grateful for :

1.

2.

3.

THIS EVENING, I am grateful for :

1.

2.

3.

DAY 20

THIS MORNING, I am grateful for :

1.

2.

3.

THIS EVENING, I am grateful for :

1.

2.

3.

DAY 21

THIS MORNING, I am grateful for :

1.

2.

3.

THIS EVENING, I am grateful for :

1.

2.

3.

DAY 22

THIS MORNING, I am grateful for :

1.

2.

3.

THIS EVENING, I am grateful for :

1.

2.

3.

DAY 23

THIS MORNING, I am grateful for :

1.

2.

3.

THIS EVENING, I am grateful for :

1.

2.

3.

DAY 24

THIS MORNING, I am grateful for :

1.

2.

3.

THIS EVENING, I am grateful for :

1.

2.

3.

DAY 25

THIS MORNING, I am grateful for :

1.

2.

3.

THIS EVENING, I am grateful for :

1.

2.

3.

DAY 26

THIS MORNING, I am grateful for :

1. _____
_____
_____

2. _____
_____
_____

3. _____
_____
_____

THIS EVENING, I am grateful for :

1. _____
_____
_____

2. _____
_____
_____

3. _____
_____
_____

DAY 27

THIS MORNING, I am grateful for :

1.

2.

3.

THIS EVENING, I am grateful for :

1.

2.

3.

DAY 28

THIS MORNING, I am grateful for :

1.

2.

3.

THIS EVENING, I am grateful for :

1.

2.

3.

DAY 29

THIS MORNING, I am grateful for :

1.

2.

3.

THIS EVENING, I am grateful for :

1.

2.

3.

DAY 30

THIS MORNING, I am grateful for :

1.

2.

3.

THIS EVENING, I am grateful for :

1.

2.

3.

················· **month 5** ·················

JOURNEY
PAGES

START
DATE :

DAY 1

THIS MORNING, I am grateful for :

1.

2.

3.

THIS EVENING, I am grateful for :

1.

2.

3.

● ●

DAY 2

THIS MORNING, I am grateful for :

1. _____

2. _____

3. _____

THIS EVENING, I am grateful for :

1. _____

2. _____

3. _____

DAY 3

THIS MORNING, I am grateful for :

1.

2.

3.

THIS EVENING, I am grateful for :

1.

2.

3.

• •

DAY 4

THIS MORNING, I am grateful for :

1.

2.

3.

THIS EVENING, I am grateful for :

1.

2.

3.

DAY 5

THIS MORNING, I am grateful for :

1.

2.

3.

THIS EVENING, I am grateful for :

1.

2.

3.

DAY 6

THIS MORNING, I am grateful for :

1.

2.

3.

THIS EVENING, I am grateful for :

1.

2.

3.

DAY 7

THIS MORNING, I am grateful for :

1.

2.

3.

THIS EVENING, I am grateful for :

1.

2.

3.

DAY 8

THIS MORNING, I am grateful for :

1.

2.

3.

THIS EVENING, I am grateful for :

1.

2.

3.

DAY 9

THIS MORNING, I am grateful for :

1.

2.

3.

THIS EVENING, I am grateful for :

1.

2.

3.

DAY 10

THIS MORNING, I am grateful for :

1. _____
_____
_____

2. _____
_____
_____

3. _____
_____
_____

THIS EVENING, I am grateful for :

1. _____
_____
_____

2. _____
_____
_____

3. _____
_____
_____

DAY 11

THIS MORNING, I am grateful for :

1.

2.

3.

THIS EVENING, I am grateful for :

1.

2.

3.

DAY 12

THIS MORNING, I am grateful for :

1.

2.

3.

THIS EVENING, I am grateful for :

1.

2.

3.

DAY 13

THIS MORNING, I am grateful for :

1.

2.

3.

THIS EVENING, I am grateful for :

1.

2.

3.

DAY 14

THIS MORNING, I am grateful for :

1.

2.

3.

THIS EVENING, I am grateful for :

1.

2.

3.

DAY 15

THIS MORNING, I am grateful for :

1.

2.

3.

THIS EVENING, I am grateful for :

1.

2.

3.

DAY 16

THIS MORNING, I am grateful for :

1.

2.

3.

THIS EVENING, I am grateful for :

1.

2.

3.

DAY 17

THIS MORNING, I am grateful for :

1.

2.

3.

THIS EVENING, I am grateful for :

1.

2.

3.

DAY 18

THIS MORNING, I am grateful for :

1.

2.

3.

THIS EVENING, I am grateful for :

1.

2.

3.

DAY 19

THIS MORNING, I am grateful for :

1.

2.

3.

THIS EVENING, I am grateful for :

1.

2.

3.

DAY 20

THIS MORNING, I am grateful for :

1.

2.

3.

THIS EVENING, I am grateful for :

1.

2.

3.

DAY 21

THIS MORNING, I am grateful for :

1.

2.

3.

THIS EVENING, I am grateful for :

1.

2.

3.

DAY 22

THIS MORNING, I am grateful for :

1.

2.

3.

THIS EVENING, I am grateful for :

1.

2.

3.

DAY 23

THIS MORNING, I am grateful for :

1.

2.

3.

THIS EVENING, I am grateful for :

1.

2.

3.

DAY 24

THIS MORNING, I am grateful for :

1.

2.

3.

THIS EVENING, I am grateful for :

1.

2.

3.

DAY 25

THIS MORNING, I am grateful for :

1.

2.

3.

THIS EVENING, I am grateful for :

1.

2.

3.

DAY 26

THIS MORNING, I am grateful for :

1.

2.

3.

THIS EVENING, I am grateful for :

1.

2.

3.

DAY 27

THIS MORNING, I am grateful for :

1.

2.

3.

THIS EVENING, I am grateful for :

1.

2.

3.

DAY 28

THIS MORNING, I am grateful for :

1.

2.

3.

THIS EVENING, I am grateful for :

1.

2.

3.

DAY 29

THIS MORNING, I am grateful for :

1.

2.

3.

THIS EVENING, I am grateful for :

1.

2.

3.

DAY 30

THIS MORNING, I am grateful for :

1.

2.

3.

THIS EVENING, I am grateful for :

1.

2.

3.

month 6

JOURNEY
PAGES

START
DATE:

DAY 1

THIS MORNING, I am grateful for :

1.

2.

3.

THIS EVENING, I am grateful for :

1.

2.

3.

DAY 2

THIS MORNING, I am grateful for :

1. _____

2. _____

3. _____

THIS EVENING, I am grateful for :

1. _____

2. _____

3. _____

DAY 3

THIS MORNING, I am grateful for :

1.

2.

3.

THIS EVENING, I am grateful for :

1.

2.

3.

DAY 4

THIS MORNING, I am grateful for :

1.

2.

3.

THIS EVENING, I am grateful for :

1.

2.

3.

DAY 5

THIS MORNING, I am grateful for :

1.

2.

3.

THIS EVENING, I am grateful for :

1.

2.

3.

DAY 6

THIS MORNING, I am grateful for :

1.

2.

3.

THIS EVENING, I am grateful for :

1.

2.

3.

DAY 7

THIS MORNING, I am grateful for :

1.

2.

3.

THIS EVENING, I am grateful for :

1.

2.

3.

DAY 8

THIS MORNING, I am grateful for :

1.

2.

3.

THIS EVENING, I am grateful for :

1.

2.

3.

DAY 9

THIS MORNING, I am grateful for :

1.

2.

3.

THIS EVENING, I am grateful for :

1.

2.

3.

DAY 10

THIS MORNING, I am grateful for :

1.

2.

3.

THIS EVENING, I am grateful for :

1.

2.

3.

DAY 11

THIS MORNING, I am grateful for :

1.

2.

3.

THIS EVENING, I am grateful for :

1.

2.

3.

DAY 12

THIS MORNING, I am grateful for :

1.

2.

3.

THIS EVENING, I am grateful for :

1.

2.

3.

DAY 13

THIS MORNING, I am grateful for :

1.

2.

3.

THIS EVENING, I am grateful for :

1.

2.

3.

DAY 14

THIS MORNING, I am grateful for :

1.

2.

3.

THIS EVENING, I am grateful for :

1.

2.

3.

DAY 15

THIS MORNING, I am grateful for :

1.

2.

3.

THIS EVENING, I am grateful for :

1.

2.

3.

DAY 16

THIS MORNING, I am grateful for :

1.

2.

3.

THIS EVENING, I am grateful for :

1.

2.

3.

DAY 17

THIS MORNING, I am grateful for :

1.

2.

3.

THIS EVENING, I am grateful for :

1.

2.

3.

DAY 18

THIS MORNING, I am grateful for :

1. _____

2. _____

3. _____

THIS EVENING, I am grateful for :

1. _____

2. _____

3. _____

DAY 19

THIS MORNING, I am grateful for :

1.

2.

3.

THIS EVENING, I am grateful for :

1.

2.

3.

DAY 20

THIS MORNING, I am grateful for :

1.

2.

3.

THIS EVENING, I am grateful for :

1.

2.

3.

DAY 21

THIS MORNING, I am grateful for :

1.

2.

3.

THIS EVENING, I am grateful for :

1.

2.

3.

DAY 22

THIS MORNING, I am grateful for :

1.

2.

3.

THIS EVENING, I am grateful for :

1.

2.

3.

DAY 23

THIS MORNING, I am grateful for :

1.

2.

3.

THIS EVENING, I am grateful for :

1.

2.

3.

DAY 24

THIS MORNING, I am grateful for :

1. _____

2. _____

3. _____

THIS EVENING, I am grateful for :

1. _____

2. _____

3. _____

DAY 25

THIS MORNING, I am grateful for :

1.

2.

3.

THIS EVENING, I am grateful for :

1.

2.

3.

DAY 26

THIS MORNING, I am grateful for :

1.

2.

3.

THIS EVENING, I am grateful for :

1.

2.

3.

DAY 27

THIS MORNING, I am grateful for :

1.

2.

3.

THIS EVENING, I am grateful for :

1.

2.

3.

DAY 28

THIS MORNING, I am grateful for :

1.

2.

3.

THIS EVENING, I am grateful for :

1.

2.

3.

DAY 29

THIS MORNING, I am grateful for :

1.

2.

3.

THIS EVENING, I am grateful for :

1.

2.

3.

DAY 30

THIS MORNING, I am grateful for :

1.

2.

3.

THIS EVENING, I am grateful for :

1.

2.

3.

about the author
— DUANE ALLEY —

TRAINER | AUTHOR | SPEAKER | COACH

Duane Alley spent the first 15 years of his professional life working with some of the biggest and fastest growing retail and franchise businesses in the country; he then spent 5 years as Head Trainer & Coach for one of the biggest Personal Development companies on the planet.

He has combined his extensive experience from the business world in delivering real world results with his success and study of personal development, rapid human change and shifting consciousness.

As a Master Trainer, Author, Speaker and Performance Coach he now works with businesses and entrepreneurs quickly and easily improve their businesses and make more money and with individuals, couples and families to make simple changes and take small steps to live better lives day by day.

KEEP IN TOUCH:

- www.duanealley.com
- www.facebook.com/duanealleypage
- www.twitter.com/DuaneAlley
- www.youtube.com/duanealley
- success@duanealley.com

GET THE COMPLETE 7 SECRETS SERIES!

VISIT DUANE ALLEY TRAINING ONLINE STORE:

www.DuaneAlley.com

Simple steps to survive the stressful situations of everyday life

Learn how to notice and fight the signs of burnout and the blues even before they take hold!

GET A COPY OF THE BOOK

for yourself or a friend in need of guidance!

www.DuaneAlley.com

three days to focus
on making the next year of your life
the best year of your life so far

| MINDSET | STRATEGY | ACTION | RESULT |

Life AND *Destiny* PRIVATE RETREAT

During the *Life & Destiny Private Retreat*, I will lead you through discovering exactly what will increase the passion, power and excitement in your life. I will help you to determine precisely which goals and achievements will turn the next 12 months into your best 12 months ever.

Then, you will learn how to make your goals come alive. Real life tested and tried strategies and tactics will help you in taking the time you need, gaining the focus you want and creating the life you will love in order to achieve and succeed.

The retreat is held exclusively for <u>only 10 people</u> at a time in an ideal mountain location that works perfectly to enhance the experience.

want to know more?
Click here for information on The Life & Destiny Private Retreat.

DUANEALLEY.COM/LIFE-DESTINY-RETREAT/

NOTES

www.ingramcontent.com/pod-product-compliance
Lightning Source LLC
Chambersburg PA
CBHW020107020526
44112CB00033B/1084